Effective Writing for Global Communication

Email, Paragraph, and Essay

JN102656

Kazumichi Enokida

Walter Davies

Fuyuko Takita

EIHŌSHA

SOUND
DOWNLOAD

テキストの音声は、弊社 HP　https://www.eihosha.co.jp/
の「テキスト音声ダウンロード」のバナーからダウンロードできます。
また、下記 QR コードを読み込み、音声ファイルをダウンロードするか、
ストリーミングページにジャンプして音声を聴くことができます。

本書について

　『グローバル・コミュニケーションのためのライティング – E メール・パラグラフ・エッセイ』は、学生の皆さんの経験や関心に基づいたライティング活動を通じて、様々なジャンルの英文の書き方を学べるよう作られた教科書です。

　本書の特徴は、E メール、パラグラフ、エッセイという、日常生活およびビジネスやアカデミックの場面で必要とされる３種類のライティングをこの１冊で学べる点です。E メールでは、フォーマルとインフォーマルの使い分け、依頼や招待などを英語で行うための方法などを取り上げます。パラグラフ・ライティングでは、トピックセンテンスを中心としたパラグラフ構成により、短く明快な文章で情報を伝達する方法を学びます。さらに本書の後半では、パラグラフ・ライティングで学んだことを発展させ、複数のパラグラフから成るエッセイ・ライティングの練習を行います。パラグラフやエッセイでは、問題解決、助言、過去の振り返りなど、様々な種類の文章が扱われています。

　また本書のもう一つの特徴として、英語ライティング能力測定のための外部検定試験、特に TOEIC® Writing Test の出題形式に対応しています。各ユニットでは写真描写問題の形式で英文を書く練習を行います。また E メール作成問題および意見記述問題も本書で取り扱われています。これらの形式の問題をさらに練習できるよう、２つの復習用ユニットが設けられています。

　本書の作成にあたり、英宝社の佐々木元社長、下村幸一氏、高野雄一郎氏に深く感謝申し上げます。

筆　　者

各ユニットの構成

Warm-up	ウォームアップとして、ユニットのテーマに関連する写真描写問題とディスカッションを行います。
Language Focus	ユニットに関連する語彙・文法を整理します。
Writing Example	モデル英文を読み、ユニットのテーマに基づく英文作成のポイントを理解します。
Preparing to Write	ライティングタスクが提示されます。書く前の準備活動として、ディスカッションによりアイデアを出し合い、これから書く英文の要点をまとめます。
Writing Practice	Preparing to Write で準備した内容をもとに、英文を書きます。
Resource Page	学生と教員の参照用に、ユニットの要点が日本語で記されています。英語版は巻末にあります。

About This Book

This textbook is designed for students who wish to develop their writing skills over a range of genres. The writing tasks themselves are student-centered, allowing students to draw from their own experiences and interests. Reading passages are provided that can be used for analysis and as examples for the writing tasks. Each unit has been primarily written in English, and can be taught either monolingually or bilingually, allowing for a flexibility of teaching approach. Supporting notes are provided both in Japanese and English, highlighting some of the key points of each genre.

The book integrates units on email writing, paragraph writing, and essay writing. The email units are designed to illustrate key aspects of email, such as formal and informal openings and closings, as well as different language functions such as requests and invitations. The paragraph writing units are designed to help students write short clear information, with topic sentences, supporting sentences and closing sentences. The essay units build from the paragraph units, so that students can develop their skills in writing linked paragraphs. The paragraph and essay units cover a range of genres from problems-solution writing to reflective writing.

The textbook has also been designed to help students with international tests of English, particularly TOEIC® Writing: Warm-up tasks in each unit require students to write sentence-length descriptions of pictures, and the email units and the opinion essay unit cover the other sections of the test. Review units provide further opportunities to practice.

Key Sections of Each Main Unit

Warm-up: This contains a picture description task and discussion questions on the main theme of the unit.

Language Focus: Two tasks (A and B) focus on key vocabulary or grammar relevant to the unit.

Writing Example: A model passage is presented with a table for analysis, providing input before output tasks.

Preparing to Write: This includes the directions for the writing task, questions for discussion to encourage the sharing of ideas, and a table for planning.

Writing Practice: A page is provided for the main writing task of the unit.

Resource Page: This provides supporting notes to the unit as a reference for both students and teacher.

Table of Contents

1. Studying Abroad

In this unit, you are going to:
- write an email about yourself
- study both formal and informal email styles

Warm-up
Picture Description

1. stand/screen

2. student/raise

Write one sentence describing each picture. Use the two words under each picture. You may change the forms.

1._____

2._____

Discussion

Discuss the following questions and write answers.

1. What different technologies do you use to communicate?

2. What are the advantages and disadvantages of writing an email?

3. When do you write email messages in your daily life?

4. Talk about the last time you wrote an email in English.

5. What is difficult for you when you write an email in English?

Language Focus

A. Choose the best answer. Each one should be used only once.

From: komatsu2001@kafuwamail.com
   To: kjones1738@kafuwamail.com
Subject: About myself

Dear Mr. Jones,

I am one of the students in your writing class on Tuesday at 10:30, and I am writing my (1)_____ introduction as you (2)_____.

I am a first-year student in the (3)_____ of Economics, and I am excited about taking your English class. At school, I studied English for six years, but I did not do so much writing in English. I (4)_____ really like to (5)_____ my writing and speaking skills. I hope to study English abroad while I am at the university.

I am from Takamatsu in Kagawa (6)_____. Do you know Kagawa? It is on Shikoku, and is famous for its Ritsurin Garden and Takamatsu Castle.

I am interested in baseball and music. At high school, I was a (7)_____ of the school baseball team, and I played the Spanish guitar. At university, I want to start a rock band.

Kind (8)_____,

Koji Matsuhiko

(a) member	(b) Faculty	(c) self	(d) Prefecture	(e) regards
(f) improve	(g) requested	(h) would		

B. Look at the greetings and closings in the box. Write "F" for formal and "I" for informal phrases.

Greetings: Hi Jim ( )   Dear Mr. Jones ( )   Hello Jane ( )
   Dear Anne ( )   Dear Sir/Madam ( )

Closings: Yours truly ( )   Yours ( )   Love ( )   Sincerely yours ( )
   Yours sincerely ( )   Take care ( )   Thanks ( )
   Yours faithfully ( )   Cheers ( )   See you ( )

Writing Example

Read and listen to the email message. Make notes in the table.

From: Yoshi777@kafuwamail.com
To: hfonda1121@kafuwamail.com
Subject: Hello from Japan

Dear Mr. and Mrs. Fonda,

Hello from Hiroshima, Japan! I will be staying at your house for three weeks from August 10th. I would like to thank you for accepting me as a homestay student.

I'm from Osaka, but now I live in Higashi-Hiroshima City, Japan. I am a first-year student at Hiroshima University, majoring in engineering. Higashi-Hiroshima is located to the east of Hiroshima City. It is called the capital of Japanese sake because it has a lot of sake breweries.

I like playing basketball. I belonged to the basketball club in my high school, and I sometimes enjoy playing basketball with my college friends. I have studied English for six years, but I am not good at speaking English. I would like to improve my English by communicating with you a lot!

As this is my first time to study in the USA, I am so excited. I hope I can study a lot of English and learn about American culture during my homestay.

I am looking forward to hearing from you.

Regards,

Yoshiki

Greeting	
Self introduction *e.g. hometown, major*	
Closing	

Preparing to Write

You are going to study abroad. Write an email reply to the following.

From: yoonji0808@kafuwamail.com
To: studentXXX1533@kafuwamail.com
Subject: Hello from South Korea
Hello! My name is Park Yoon-Ji. I'm from South Korea. You and I have been assigned to be roommates in a student apartment for next school year at Cal State, LA. Please call me Yoon-Ji. I graduated from a high school in Busan this winter, and I am now at a language school in Busan, preparing for next year. I'm going to major in economics. I like listening to music and cooking—I hope I can cook some Korean dishes for us. Please feel free to email me to figure out who's bringing what to our room! Best, Yoon-Ji PS I also have a Messenger account. It's @yoonji0808.

Work in a pair. Ask and answer the following questions.

1. Where are you from?
2. What is your major?
3. What are your hobbies and interests?
4. What do you want to ask Yoon-Ji?
5. How are you going to start the email?
6. How are you going to finish the email?
7. Is there anything else you want to write in your email?

Make notes in the table.

Greeting	
Self introduction	
Closing	

Write your email on the next page.

Writing Practice

From: studentXXX1533@kafuwamail.com
To: yoonji0808@kafuwamail.com
Subject: RE: Hello from South Korea

_____

_____

_____

_____

_____

_____

_____

_____

_____

_____

_____

_____

_____

Work in a pair. Pass your email messages to each other. Write a comment (e.g. "I have the same hobby as you ...").

_____

_____

_____

Resource Page

メールの作法：フォーマルとインフォーマルの使い分け

　大学生活、社会生活、仕事において、メールは他人と連絡を取るための重要な手段です。ですからメールを書く時にはフォーマルとインフォーマルのどちらの文体で書くか決めておきましょう。インフォーマルな文体はルールが比較的自由で、短縮形や、短く不完全な語句が使われます。フォーマルなメールは、全体の構成が明確で、省略のない完全な文が用いられます。

　書き出しと結びを見れば、そのメールがフォーマルかインフォーマルかわかります。インフォーマルなメールでは、Hello / Hi の後にファーストネームを組み合わせた挨拶が使われます。フォーマルなメールでは、Dear とファミリーネームの組み合わせが使われます。

　フォーマルなメールの結びは、国によって若干異なります。米国のビジネスメールでは Yours truly や Sincerely yours が使われるのに対し、英国のフォーマルな場面では Yours sincerely が使われます。Dear Sir/Madam で始まるような大変改まったメールでは、結びに Yours faithfully が使われます。

　結びの語の中には、フォーマルとインフォーマルの両方で用いられるものもあります。よく使われるのは Kind regards と Best wishes の二つです。

Summary in English on p. 83

About Japan: *Work with a partner and explain the picture.*
(Hint: What do you know about Himeji Castle?)

2. Festivals

In this unit, you are going to:
- write a descriptive paragraph of a festival
- study the structure of a descriptive paragraph

Warm-up

<u>Picture Description</u>

1. dance/near

2. women/along

Write one sentence describing each picture. Use the two words under each picture. You may change the forms.

1._____

2._____

<u>Discussion</u>

Discuss the following questions and write answers.

1. What are three famous festivals in Japan?

2. What are two world-famous festivals outside of Japan?

3. Describe the *Obon* Dance Festival to your partner.

4. What are the good points of having festivals?

5. What do people do at your annual university festival?

A. Choose the best answer. Each one should be used only once.

Summer Festivals in Japan

Some of the most attractive Japanese traditional events are the summer festivals (1)_____ *Natsu Matsuri,* which are held (2)_____ the country. These wonderful events, such as the (3)_____ Sumida River Fireworks in Tokyo, are enjoyed by foreign tourists, particularly during July and August. A major (4)_____ event is the *Nebuta* Festival, which is (5) _____ in Aomori Prefecture. The festival features huge floats called *Nebuta,* on which there are (6)_____ figures of warriors. There are also dancers who wear special costumes called *Haneto.* *Natsu Matsuri* such as the Sumida River Fireworks and the Nebuta Festival (7)_____ millions of people every year.

(a) attract　(b) one of the biggest　(c) spectacular　(d) mythical
(e) across　(f) regional　(g) called

Underline the topic sentence and concluding sentence of this paragraph.

B. Describe these festivals in one sentence in English.

1. *Sendai Tanabata Festival* （仙台七夕祭り）

_____

2. *Kyoto Gion Festival* （京都祇園祭り）

_____

3. *Yosakoi Festival* （よさこい祭り）

_____

4. *Awaodori* （阿波踊り）

_____

Writing Example

Read and listen to the paragraph. Make notes in the table.

Hogmanay

Hogmanay takes place at New Year, and is an important Scottish festival. The word "Hogmanay" may come from sixteenth century French, meaning either "a gift at New Year" or just "New Year". In big cities like Edinburgh, there is often a fireworks display. "First footing" is part of the celebration; the first person to visit a house at midnight usually brings a black bun, made of rye bread, and a piece of coal as gifts. These symbolize having enough food and keeping the house warm in the new year. In the small town of Stonehaven on the east coast of Scotland, there is also the tradition of fireball swinging at New Year. Local people make large balls of wire that contain paper and wood, and attach the balls to chains. At midnight, they set fire to the balls, walk down the main street to the harbor, and throw the fireballs into the sea. Traditional events at Hogmanay encourage people to start the New Year with warm hearts.

Name of the festival	
Meaning of the name	
Location	
Date	
What people do	**Notes** *Watch a fireworks display*

Underline the topic sentence and concluding sentence of this paragraph.

Preparing to Write

Choose a Japanese festival that you want to write about.

Work in a pair. Discuss the following questions.

1. What is the Japanese name of the festival? Explain the meaning in English.
2. Is it a local or a national festival?
3. What does the festival celebrate?
4. Where does it take place?
5. What happens in the festival?
6. What equipment is needed?
7. Do people wear anything special?
8. Do people eat or drink anything special?

Make notes in the table.

Name of the festival	
Meaning of the name	
Location	
Date	
What people do	Notes

Write your topic sentence for your paragraph.

_____

_____

Write about the festival on the next page.

Writing Practice

A Japanese Festival

_____

_____

_____

_____

_____

_____

_____

_____

_____

_____

_____

_____

_____

_____

_____

_____

_____

_____

_____

_____

_____

Work in a pair. Pass your festival descriptions to each other. Write a comment (e.g. "We have a similar festival in our prefecture called …").

_____

_____

_____

Resource Page

Summary in English on p. 83

About Japan: *Work with a partner and explain the picture.*
(Hint: What do you know about Kagura?)

3. Movies

In this unit, you are going to:
- write a short review of your favorite movie
- study some genres and key terms used in reviews

Warm-up
Picture Description

1. popcorn/laugh

2. couple/at

Write one sentence describing each picture. Use the two words under each picture. You may change the forms.

1._____

2._____

Discussion

Discuss the following questions and write answers.

1. What kinds of movies do you like to watch?

2. Can you name five famous comedies?

3. Can you name five famous action movies?

4. Which is your favorite movie, and why?

5. Describe your favorite movie in one minute.

A. Choose the best answer. Each one should be used only once.

> ## Movie Review
>
> 'Star Wars' is a famous (1)_____ movie and is about the struggle between good and evil, friendship, and sacrifice. The story (2)_____ in a distant galaxy many years in the past. The (3)_____ is Luke Skywalker, a young farmer who accidentally receives an emergency message from a princess. It is for a jedi knight called Obi Wan Kenobi, asking him to take the robots to another planet because they contain information about a space station, the Death Star, that has a terror weapon. After Luke's uncle and aunt (4)_____, he and Obi Wan set out on the mission. Luke has to (5)_____ his self-doubt and is eventually able to rescue the princess and destroy the Death Star. I (6)_____ this movie because it has a classic (7)_____, which is often used for myths and epic stories, it has many comic moments, and it is also visually stimulating with many interesting (8)_____. George Lucas, who directed the movie (9)_____ by Akira Kurosawa's 'The Hidden Fortress'. In terms of movie history, 'Star Wars' had a major impact on audiences and film makers.

(a) overcome	(b) main character	(c) recommend	(d) was influenced
(e) is set	(f) plot	(g) science fantasy	(h) are murdered	(i) sets

Underline the topic sentence and concluding sentence of this paragraph.

Match the movie descriptions with their genres.

1. A flesh-eating monster slowly hunts down the crew of a container ship. _____	a) action movie
2. A young princess defeats an evil lord using the magic of a good wizard. _____	b) horror movie
3. A spaceship crashes on Mars, and the crew are helped by friendly aliens. ____	c) drama
4. Three men crash their plane and use their skills to return home to their families. _____	d) science fiction movie
5. a racing driver is chased by gangsters, but escapes by driving across the desert, flying a helicopter, and using a speedboat. _____	e) adventure movie
6. 6. an old man returns to his hometown to re-connect with his brother. _____	f) fantasy movie

Writing Example

Read and listen to the movie review. Make notes in the table.

My Favorite Movie

'The Godfather' is a famous gangster movie, and is about love, loyalty, and betrayal in a Mafia family. The movie is mainly set in New York in the mid 1940s, just after the Second World War. The main character is Michael Corleone, who is the son of Vito Corleone, the head of a powerful New York crime family. Vito is known as 'The Godfather'. Michael is a war hero who does not want to be a gangster. However, when Vito is shot and badly wounded by a rival crime organization, Michael returns to defend his father, and eventually becomes head of the crime family. I recommend this film because, in addition to being a gangster movie, it is also about very difficult family relationships, particularly between Michael, his brothers, his sister, and his father. The movie won three Academy Awards (Oscars), made Al Pacino famous, and remains one of the most famous movies ever made.

Movie Name	
Themes	
Setting of the story	
Time period	
Main character	
Story	
Writer's opinion of the movie	
Other information	

Underline the topic sentence and concluding sentence of this paragraph.

Preparing to Write

You are going to write a paragraph about your favorite movie.
Work in a pair. Ask and answer the following questions.

1. What is your favorite movie?

2. Where and when is the movie set?

3. Who are the main characters?

4. What is the story about?

5. What is the main theme (e.g. love)?

6. Why is it your favorite movie?

7. What else do you know about the movie?

Write down the key information.

Movie Name	
Themes	
Setting of the story	
Time period	
Main character	
Story	
Your opinion of the movie	
Other information	

Write your topic sentence for your paragraph.

_____

_____

Write about your favorite movie on the next page.

Writing Practice

My Favorite Movie

_____
_____
_____
_____
_____
_____
_____
_____
_____
_____
_____
_____
_____
_____
_____
_____
_____
_____
_____
_____

Work in a pair. Pass your reviews to each other. Write a comment (e.g. "I also enjoyed this movie …").

_____
_____
_____

Resource Page

映画のレビュー（紹介文、論評）の書き方
　このユニットでは、皆さんの好きな映画について英語で書いてみましょう。映画のレビューを書く際には、**ジャンル**、**テーマ**、**ストーリー**と**プロット**、およびその作品についての皆さんの意見、以上がポイントとなります。

1) **ジャンル**：ジャンルにはいろいろな種類がありますが、最も人気のあるものはアクション映画、コメディ（ラブコメを含む）、犯罪/ギャング映画、ホラー映画、ミュージカル、SF、ファンタジー映画です。
2) **テーマ**：愛、死、権力、生存、偏見など、作品の中心となる概念です。
3) **ストーリー**と**プロット**：ストーリーは作中のできごとを**時間順**に説明したもので、プロットは作中のできごとを**登場順**に説明したものです。

＊映画のレビューでは、作中のできごとを説明する際に現在形が用いられます。

Summary in English on p. 84

About Japan: *Work with a partner and explain the picture.*
(Hint: What do you know about Totoro?)

4. Campus Life

In this unit you are going to:
- write a request email
- learn useful vocabulary and terms for university study

Warm-up

Picture Description

1. hold/shelf   2. young/look

Write one sentence describing each picture. Use the two words under each picture. You may change the forms.

1._____

2._____

Discussion

Discuss the following questions and write answers.

1. What courses are you studying this semester?

2. What subjects do you want to study most this year, and why?

3. When do you need to communicate by email with your teachers?

4. Describe the last time you gave or got help from other students (e.g., the content of lectures, computer programs, etc.).

5. Describe the last time you asked a teacher for help.

Language Focus

A. Choose the best answer. Each one should be used only once.

From: Linda777@kafuwamail.com

   To: bjones0464@kafuwamail.com

Subject: Could I borrow a book?

Hi Brian,

How's (1) _____? I have a quick question and (2) _____. I
(3) _____ that you were talking about a book called *The Secret History
of Costaguana*. If you have the book, (4) _____ borrow it for a couple
of days? I'm (5) _____ a paper for my Latin American Literature
course, and I found a reference to the book in some literary criticism that I
want to quote from. I just need to (6) _____ my discussion on the
influence of European literature on Latin America is correct. I'll return it to
you (7) _____ I'm finished with my paper. Thanks (8) _____!

Take care,

Linda

(a) check if   (b) everything   (c) may I   (d) request   (e) in advance
(f) working on   (g) remember   (h) as soon as

B. Write the correct words next to the definitions.

1. to repeat or copy out words from another text: _____

2. an academic essay or article: _____

3. someone who has completed their first university degree: _____

4. article section where the writer develops the key themes: _____

5. mention of a book or article: _____

6. the analysis and evaluation of fiction and non-fiction: _____

(a) discussion   (b) quote   (c) paper   (d) literary criticism
(e) reference   (f) graduate

Writing Example

Read and listen to the email message. Make notes in the table.

From: risasa@kafuwamail.com
To: lizang@kafuwamail.com
Subject: Could you check my draft?
Dear Professor Ng,
.
I am Rina Sasaki, a fourth-year student in your class 'Globalism and World Peace'. I am planning to study at a graduate school in Canada next year to study more about global peace and international development. I have decided to do so because I was so inspired by your course. I have just finished writing my statement of purpose in English for my grad school application. Would you be able to read it and give me any suggestions to improve it?
I am looking forward to hearing from you.
Yours sincerely,
Rina Sasaki

Greeting	
Background/reason for the request	
Request question/statement	
Closing	

Preparing to Write

Ms. Smith (msmith@kafuwamail.com), your English teacher, has lots of fiction and non-fiction books in her office. She has offered to lend them to students. You want to visit her office to borrow a book from her.

Work in a pair. Discuss the following questions.

1. What is your grade (e.g., freshman, sophomore)?
2. What is your major?
3. What is your level of English (e.g., beginner, pre-intermediate)?
4. What do you like reading (e.g. novels, short stories, comics)?
5. When can you visit Ms. Smith's office?
6. When and how will you return the book?
7. What do you want to write in the subject line of the email?

Make notes in the table.

Greeting	
Background/reason for the request	
Request question/statement	
Closing	

Write the 'Subject' line of your email.

Subject:

Write your email on the next page.

Writing Practice

From:
To:
Subject:

_____

_____

_____

_____

_____

_____

_____

_____

_____

_____

_____

_____

_____

_____

Work in a pair. Pass your email messages to each other. Write a comment (e.g. "I'm interested in the same kind of fiction …").

_____

_____

_____

Resource Page

依頼のメール

　授業中に他の学生に物を借りたい場合や、先生に教室の温度を調節してもらいたい場合など、依頼は日常生活で頻繁に行われます。依頼には多くの表現があるので、丁寧さの度合いに応じて適切な表現を選びましょう。

　依頼における丁寧さの度合いは二つの点を考えて決めます。一つは自分と依頼を行う相手との立場の違い、そしてもう一つは依頼の「大きさ」です。例えば先生に窓を開けてほしいと頼むのは、その立場にある相手への依頼ですからさほど難しくありません。一方、語学留学のために書いた英文願書のチェックを先生に依頼するような場合、これは時間を要する作業ですから、丁寧さの度合いの高い表現を用いる必要があります。

　依頼の表現には様々なものがあります。I would be grateful if you could … （…していただけましたら幸いです）のような平叙文もありますが、多くは疑問文の形を取ります。これは依頼の可否を相手の意思に委ねるためです。依頼された相手は、承諾するか断るかの返事を求められることになります。

　通常、依頼の表現には法助動詞（can / may / will）を使います。過去形（could / would / might）の方が丁寧さの度合いが上です。例えば Could I …?（…してもよろしいでしょうか）は Can I …?（…してもいい？）よりも丁寧です。丁寧さの度合いの高い依頼表現としては以下のものがあります。

　Would it be possible for you to…?

　Would you be able to…?

　I am wondering if you could….

Summary in English on p. 84

About Japan: *Work with a partner and explain the picture.*
(Hint: What do you know about Murasaki Shikibu?)

5. Environment

In this unit, you are going to:
- write a problem-solution paragraph
- study terms relating to causes and effects

Warm-up
Picture Description

1. solar panel/on   2. firefighters/in front of

Write one sentence describing each picture. Use the two words under each picture. You may change the forms.

1._____

2._____

Discussion

Discuss the following questions and write answers.

1. What environmental problems have you watched on the news recently?

2. What is global warming?

3. What are some of the effects of global warming?

4. How can governments act to improve the environment?

5. How do you try to be environmentally friendly?

Language Focus

A. Choose the best answer. Each one should be used only once.

> ### Global Warming
>
> Global warming, the (1)_____ in the average (2)_____ of the Earth, is a major (3)_____. The warming of the planet has led to rising sea levels and changes in weather (4)_____. This has resulted in the more frequent occurrence of (5)_____ weather events such as major flooding, hurricanes, and heatwaves. Human activity has contributed to global warming through the (6)_____ of greenhouse gases such as carbon dioxide. These are produced in the (7)_____ and use of fossil fuels, such as coal, oil, and gas. One way of reducing greenhouse gas emissions is to replace fossil fuels with (8)_____ energy sources such as solar power. This change will have major long-term benefits both for energy security in many countries as well as reducing levels of (9)_____ around the world.

(a) pollution	(b) extraction	(c) temperature	(d) extreme
(e) renewable	(f) emission	(g) rise	(h) patterns	(i) problem

B. Choose the best answer. Each one should be used only once.

1. _____ to global warming, the temperature of the Earth's surface is rising.

2. _____ of heavy deforestation, the rate of desertification is increasing in Saharan Africa.

3. As _____ the heavy precipitation, several neighborhoods experienced severe flooding.

4. There has been no rain for over three months in this area. _____, people in the village cannot grow crops and are experiencing food shortage.

(a) a result of	(b) therefore	(c) because	(d) due

Writing Example

SOUND DOWNLOAD

Read and listen to the paragraph. Make notes in the table.

Environmentally-friendly Tea

Many of us like to drink tea, but the way we make it or buy it can affect the environment. We often buy teabags or bottled tea, but this adds to the environmental problem of plastic waste. Teabags are usually sold in boxes covered in cellophane, they are often individually wrapped, and many teabags actually contain plastic to give them strength. If we buy bottled tea, the bottles are usually made of plastic and have labels made of cellophane. Consequently, buying teabags and bottled tea adds to the problem of plastic in our garbage. One solution to this problem is to buy loose-leaf tea and use a teapot. This is a more traditional way of making tea and adds to the flavor. Also, instead of buying bottles of tea, you can cool the tea in a refrigerator and use a thermos flask. Once the tea has been made, the tea leaves can be used as compost in plant pots or in gardens. By making tea in this way the amount of plastic waste is greatly reduced.

Problem	Tea bags:
	Bottled tea:
Solution	

Underline the topic sentence and concluding sentence.

Preparing to Write

You are going to write about environmentally-friendly shopping.
Write down all the items that you buy in a month.

Work in a pair. Discuss the following questions.

1. Where do you go shopping?
2. How do you get to the shops?
3. How do you pack the things you buy?
4. What are some of the problems with the cleaning items that you buy?
5. What are some of the problems with the food that you buy?
6. What are some of the problems with the toiletries (e.g. shampoo) that you buy?
7. What are some solutions to the problems?

Make notes in the table.

Problem	
Solution	

Write your topic sentence.

_____

_____

Write your concluding sentence.

_____

_____

Write your paragraph on the next page.

Writing Practice

Environmentally-friendly Shopping

_____

_____

_____

_____

_____

_____

_____

_____

_____

_____

_____

_____

_____

_____

_____

_____

_____

_____

Work in a pair. Pass your paragraphs to each other. Write a comment (e.g. "That's a good idea. I'll try it …").

_____

_____

_____

Resource Page

Summary in English on p. 85

About Japan: *Work with a partner and explain the picture.*
(Hint: What do you know about typhoons?)

6. Lifestyle

In this unit, you are going to:
- write a paragraph giving advice
- study some key phrases for giving advice

Warm-up
Picture Description

1. prepare/together   2. for/papers

Write one sentence describing each picture. Use the two words under each picture. You may change the forms.

1._____

2._____

Discussion

Discuss the following questions and write answers.

1. When was the last time you gave someone some advice? What was it?

2. If you need advice, who do you usually ask?

3. What was the best advice you ever received from a teacher?

4. What was the best advice you received from another student?

5. How often do you read advice (e.g. "Tips for staying Healthy") on the Internet or in magazines?

Language Focus

A. Choose the best answer. Each one should be used only once.

> ## Tips for Cooking
>
> If you live a busy life, saving time on cooking is important, and there are several good ways of achieving this. For example, (1)_____ salads and vegetables (2)_____ meat saves you time. This is because you only need to wash your kitchen knife and chopping board once. Make the salad first, then chop the vegetables, and finally chop the meat. Another way of saving time is filling your washing bowl early. You (3)_____ fill it with soapy water before cooking. (4)_____ you prepare food and (5)_____ cooking, you can (6)_____ dirty dishes and utensils immediately in the water. (7)_____ let food and sauces dry out on plates and in pots. (8)_____, they will stick, making cleaning much harder. By making small changes in your approach to cooking, you can free up a lot of time for other activities such as studying.

(a) start	(b) before	(c) place	(d) as	(e) preparing	(f) should
(g) don't	(h) otherwise				

B. Choose the best answer. Each one should be used only once.

1. If I _____ you, I'd spend more time on studying.

2. You _____ train harder if want to get to the final.

3. _____ start your hike without warm clothes and a waterproof coat.

4. _____ a good breakfast. It will help you concentrate in the morning.

5. If I _____ been prepared for bad weather, I would have been in trouble.

(a) don't	(b) hadn't	(c) have	(d) should	(e) were

Writing Example

Read and listen to the paragraph. Make notes in the table.

Staying Organized

These days, we all lead very busy lives, and it's easy to lose track of what needs to be done. Being well organized is a key to success, and this can be achieved by using some simple techniques such as making a to-do list and avoiding piles of paper. A to-do list is a good way of making sure that you complete your tasks. At the start of the day, write down all the tasks that you need to complete. When you complete a task, cross it off the list. If anything is left at the end of the day, write it on the following day's to-do list. Another example is avoiding piles of paper, which is an important way of keeping your workspace tidy. If a sheet of paper is not important, throw it away immediately. At the end of the day, make sure that all important papers are filed properly so that you can start the new day easily with a clear workspace. If you are well-organized, you can deal with challenges much more effectively, and this will make you calmer and more relaxed in your daily life.

Example 1	benefit
Example 2	benefit

Underline the topic sentence and the concluding sentence.

Preparing to Write

You are going to write an advice column on "studying English effectively".
Work in a pair. Ask and answer the following questions.

1. Why is studying English important?

2. What is difficult about studying English?

3. How do you learn new words?

4. What advice do you have for practicing reading?

5. What advice do you have for practicing writing?

6. What advice do you have for practicing listening?

7. What advice do you have for practicing speaking?

Think about two key techniques for studying English effectively and make notes.

Technique 1	benefit
Technique 2	benefit

Write your topic sentence.

_____

_____

Write your concluding sentence.

_____

_____

Write your advice column on the next page.

Writing Practice

Studying English Effectively

(blank lined writing space)

Work in a pair. Pass your reviews to each other. Write a comment (e.g. "I also repeat words to myself ...").

Resource Page

Summary in English on p. 85

About Japan: *Work with a partner and explain the picture.*
(Hint: What do you know about Marie Kondo?)

Review (1)

Look at the following writing tasks. Choose one email message and one paragraph. Circle the numbers that you choose, and write about the topics. Refer back to the previous units for useful information.

Email Options
1. Write an email to your teacher about your travel experiences in Japan (or abroad).
2. Write a request email to your teacher for help and information about an English test such as TOEIC, TOEFL, or IELTS.

Paragraph Options
3. Write a descriptive paragraph about your country's traditional music.
4. Write a review paragraph of your favorite novel or short story.
5. Write a problem-solution paragraph on improving your university cafeteria at lunchtime.
6. Write an advice paragraph about staying healthy.

| From: |
| To: |
| Subject: |
| |

Paragraph: _____

About Japan: *Write a sentence describing the picture.*

---

7. Sport

In this unit you are going to:
- write an invitation email
- write a reply to an invitation email (acceptance or refusal)
- study the features of an invitation email (formal and informal)

Warm-up
Picture Description

1. bow/on	2. play/trees

Write one sentence describing each picture. Use the two words under each picture. You may change the forms.

1._____

2._____

Discussion

Discuss the following questions and write answers.

1. Describe how you keep fit during the week.

2. What sports do you like to watch or play?

3. What was the last leisure event you attended? How did you get there?

4. If you invited someone to a baseball game, what would you say in English?

5. What is the hardest thing about writing an invitation email?

Language Focus

Choose the best answer. Each one should be used only once.

From: Tanak33@kafuwamail.com
   To: WRSmith@kafuwamail.com
Subject: Invitation to speak at a symposium

Dear Professor Smith,

I am writing (1)_____ the Center for Global Studies at Kurosawa University. We are (2)_____ in your work on intercultural communication in sports teams and (3)_____ invite you to speak at our symposium on 1st September next year. The theme of the symposium is 'Language and Teamwork'. It takes place in the afternoon, and you would be one of three speakers.

We (4)_____ hearing from you.

Yours truly,

Haruko Tanaka

From: WRSmith@kafuwamail.com
   To: Tanak33@kafuwamail.com
Subject: RE: Invitation to speak at a symposium

Dear Ms. Tanaka,

Thank you for your kind invitation to speak at the symposium next year. Unfortunately, I will be in South Africa during September, and so I am unable to accept your invitation. If you (5)_____ speak at your university at some other time in the future, please do not (6)_____ contact me.

I hope the symposium goes well.

Kind regards,

William Smith

| (a) look forward to | (b) on behalf of | (c) would like me to |
| (d) would like to | (e) hesitate to | (f) very interested |

Writing Example

Read and listen to the email messages. Make notes in the table.

From: kotaka1999@kafuwamail.com To: johnron2001@kafuwamail.com Subject: Judo event in Osaka
Hi John, I hope you are having a good weekend. I've just finished Professor Kagawa's homework. It took me almost three hours! Do you want to watch a judo tournament in Osaka on the last Saturday of next month? Our judo club has managed to get six tickets for the national tournament. We'll probably catch an early morning shinkansen, and come back in the evening. Can you give me an answer in the next couple of days? Take care, Koji P.S. I hope you found the homework easier than I did!
From: kotaka1999@kafuwamail.com To: johnron2001@kafuwamail.com Subject: RE: Judo event in Osaka
Hello Koji, Thanks for the invitation. Yes, that sounds great. I would love to watch some judo with you and the others. I hope it will help me improve my technique. If you let me know the cost of the ticket, I will pass you the money at the practice session on Monday evening. Cheers, John P.S. I managed to finish Professor Kagawa's homework – not easy!

Greeting	
Invitation	
Event (what/where/when)	
Closing	
Invitation accepted? (Yes/No)	

Preparing to Write

You are going to write an email exchange between yourself and another student involving an invitation to a sports event.

Write down as many sports events as you can in the box.

Choose one event for your email.

Work in a pair. Discuss the following questions.

1. What is the name of the event?

2. Is it a local or a national event?

3. What is the location of the event?

4. When is the event? What time does it start and end?

5. How do you plan to get to the event?

6. What else do you want to add to the email?

Fill out the key language for the email exchange in the table.

Greeting	
Invitation	
Information about the event	
Closing	

Write an invitation to the sporting event on the next page.

Writing Practice

From:
    To:
Subject:

_____
_____
_____
_____
_____
_____
_____
_____
_____
_____
_____
_____
_____
_____

Practice writing a reply to the invitation.

From:
    To:
Subject: RE:

_____
_____
_____
_____
_____
_____
_____
_____

Resource Page

Summary in English on p. 86

About Japan: *Work with a partner and explain the picture.*
(Hint: What do you know about sumo?)

8. Culture

In this unit you are going to:
- write a descriptive essay about your local area and culture
- study essay structure and connectors

Warm-up

Picture Description

1. opposite/tea

2. man/in front of

Write one sentence describing each picture. Use the two words under each picture. You may change the forms.

1._____

2._____

Discussion

Discuss the following questions and write answers.

1. What are the most interesting cultural sites in your hometown or prefecture?

2. Which areas of the world are you interested in visiting, and why?

3. If you wanted to explain traditional Japanese culture, what would you talk about?

4. If you wanted to explain modern Japanese culture, what would you talk about?

5. Explain a traditional Japanese dish in one minute.

Language Focus

A. Choose the best answer. Each one should be used only once.

Singapore

Strategically located on the tip of the Malay Peninsula next to the Straits of Malacca, Singapore is a small city state of (1)_____ 5.6 million people. Its diverse population, which places high value on ethnic harmony and inclusion, creates a vibrant mix of culture, which can be seen in the languages spoken within the city, and its wide range of festivals. (2)_____ the language of education is English, reflecting modern Singapore's colonial past, there are three more official languages: Mandarin, Malay, and Tamil. These are spoken by the main ethnic groups (Chinese, Malays, and Indians), so that most residents are bilingual. This rich linguistic mix benefits Singapore economically, helping with its business connections across the world, and attracting entrepreneurs to settle in the city. In (3)_____, the diverse population creates a city full of extraordinary festivals, reflecting different religions and traditions. (4)_____, the Lantern Festival takes place at the end of Chinese New Year, Hari Raya Puasa celebrates the end of Ramadan for Muslims, and Deepavali (Diwali) is the Hindu festival of light. (5)_____, at the festivals, different ethnic and religious groups mingle to enjoy the celebrations. (6)_____, Singapore's emphasis on ethnic harmony and its diverse population make it a vibrant place to visit and work.

(a) moreover (b) thus (c) around (d) for example (e) addition (f) while

B. Write the correct transitional signals to complete each sentence.

1. _____ he was very tired, the employee completed his work on time.
2. _____ the bad weather, most people arrived late for work.
3. We should preserve old buildings. _____, an important part of our heritage will be lost.
4. The athlete was suffering from a virus. _____, she performed poorly.

(a) otherwise   (b) consequently   (c) although   (d) owing to

Writing Example

Read and listen to the essay. Make notes in the table.

Montreal: 'Cultural Capital of Canada'

Situated in the Province of Quebec, Montreal is one of the oldest and most vibrant cities in Canada. With its French heritage and its ethnic diversity, two important cultural aspects of the city are its distinctive classic European-style architecture that exists alongside modern designs, and its great range of cuisine.

While there are many modern buildings, including the Montreal Biosphere, the city has maintained its architectural cultural heritage. The district of Old Montreal has the atmosphere of a classic European city center. In keeping with the French heritage there are plenty of cafes with outdoor seating, so that you can enjoy a cup of coffee or a meal while watching the world go by.

The cuisine of Montreal has a strong French influence, but there are also several homegrown dishes. An example is Montreal smoked meat, which is often served in a sandwich. In addition, the city's restaurants reflect its diverse population, serving dishes from the Caribbean, Europe, the Middle East, South Asia, and East Asia.

With its old-world atmosphere and its blend of cultures, Montreal is a unique North American city, reflected in its architecture and its population. Another cultural aspect of the city is its energetic arts scene, with music festivals, museums, galleries, and exhibitions. Its rich culture and diversity make Montreal a fascinating city to visit.

Name	
Location	
Cultural topic of paragraph 1	Topic: Examples:
Cultural topic of paragraph 2	Topic: Examples:

Underline the thesis statement in the essay.

Preparing to Write

You are going to write about your hometown or prefecture (e.g. Izumo City or Shimane Prefecture).

Write down as many cultural aspects of the area as you can in the box.

Work in a pair. Discuss the following questions.

1. Which place are you going to write about?

2. Where is it located?

3. Describe some famous sites.

4. Describe some famous dishes.

5. What are some famous products that are made there?

6. Are there any important festivals?

7. Which two cultural topics do you want to write about?

Make notes in the table.

Name	
Location	
Cultural topic of paragraph 1	Topic: Examples:
Cultural topic of paragraph 2	Topic: Examples:

Write a four-paragraph descriptive essay about your hometown or prefecture on the next page.

Writing Practice

My Hometown/Prefecture

Resource Page

エッセイの構成

タイトル：エッセイの内容を読者に明確に示すタイトルを付けます。タイトルでは、接続詞・前置詞・冠詞を除き、それぞれの単語の最初の文字をすべて大文字にします。

序論：最初の段落では、エッセイのテーマを導入した後で、エッセイの主張を端的に言い表した**主題文**（thesis statement）を書きます。主題文では、エッセイの**テーマ**と**メインアイデア**（そのテーマについて主張しようとしていること）に加え、本論で詳しく述べていく**2〜3の論点**を示します。主題文は2文に分けても構いません。

本論：序論で示した論点を2〜3段落で詳しく述べます。**1段落につき1論点**をルールとし、論点と無関係なことは書かないようにしましょう。パラグラフ・ライティングの時と同じく、各段落はトピックセンテンスで始め、残りの部分はすべてトピックセンテンスを支える**裏付け文**（supporting sentences）とします。さらにこれらのトピックセンテンスがすべて、主題文の裏付けとなるようにします。

結論：最後の段落では、エッセイの結論を示します。序論で示したメインアイデアを再述し、コメントなどを加えてエッセイをまとめます。

Summary in English on p. 86

About Japan: *Work with a partner and explain the picture.*
(Hint: What do you know about the Ryoanji rock garden?)

9. Memory

In this unit, you are going to:
- write a reflective essay about your high school days
- study useful vocabulary about learning experiences
- practice some punctuation

Warm-up
Picture Description

1. look/fish   2. uniform/next to

Write one sentence describing each picture. Use the two words under each picture. You may change the forms.

1._____

2._____

Discussion

Discuss the following questions and write answers.

1. Describe your high school.

2. Which was your best year at high school, and why?

3. What events at high school do you remember best?

4. Who were your best teachers, and why?

5. What advice would you give to students entering high school?

Language Focus

A. Choose the best answer. Each one should be used only once.

My Life at Elementary School

When I was an elementary school student, our teachers had a strong (1)_____ to our physical, intellectual, and emotional (2)_____. For example, one of the big (3)_____ of the year was the annual school sports festival, in which we all participated. This helped us to (4)_____ coordination and stamina. Many of our classroom (5)_____ were designed to help intellectually. Staff were also (6)_____ of the importance of emotional development and allowed us to express ourselves in three important areas: art, music, and writing. Consequently, my (7)_____ of elementary school was a positive one, and I (8)_____ the lessons it taught me. In the future, I would like to make the same kind of (9)_____ to education as those elementary school teachers.

(a) value   (b) development   (c) experience   (d) contribution
(e) aware   (f) commitment   (g) develop   (h) activities   (i) events

B. Choose a colon (:), semicolon (;), or comma (,) for each sentence.

1. If you see Kate tomorrow ( ) please give her this note.

2. There are three items on the menu ( ) pizza, pasta, and soup.

3. All the students are nervous ( ) the exams take place tomorrow.

4. The Deathly Hallows are three key objects ( ) a wand, a stone and a cloak.

5. The streets are empty ( ) a storm is coming.

6. When I was younger ( ) I used to play rugby.

Writing Example

Read and listen to the essay. Make notes in the table.

High School Days

School days are a time of great change, and when I think about those times, I remember various events and activities. Examples of these are sports, lunches, classes, trips, and school festivals. In particular, high school is a time where a great deal is learned from others, and two events which had a great influence on me were playing in a rugby tournament and taking university entrance examinations.

When I was at high school, I played in a rugby tournament. I had started playing rugby at elementary school, and continued to play in junior high school and high school. My school was divided into houses, and each house had a rugby team. Our team won the final of the house tournament. From this experience, I learned the importance of training, playing sport with other people, and making a commitment to a group. Playing on a team helped me to develop many friendships at that time, and to value the contribution of others.

A second important event in my life was taking university entrance examinations at the age of eighteen. Preparing for the examinations was very hard; I had to stop playing sport for several months. I was helped by a teacher who taught a class to prepare for the examinations; I learned from him how to summarize and develop ideas. This experience made me realize the importance of a good dedicated teacher.

I learned many things during my school days, although I was probably not aware of them at the time. In both playing sport and taking university entrance examinations, I learned to value the help and advice of other people, and the importance of caring for others.

Event 1	What was learned
Event 2	What was learned

Underline the thesis statement in the essay.

Preparing to Write

You are going to write an essay about some important events in your high school life and what you learned from them.

Work in a pair. Ask and answer the following questions.

1. What club activities did you do?

2. How were you involved in your school festival?

3. What subjects did you enjoy the most, and why?

4. Where did you go on vacation?

5. What did you enjoy most in your high school days?

6. Which events do you want to write about?

7. What did you learn from those events?

Make notes about the key events.

Event 1	What was learned
Event 2	What was learned

Write a thesis statement for your essay.

_____

_____

Write a four-paragraph reflective essay about your high school life on the next page.

Writing Practice

High School Days

Resource Page

過去の経験を語るエッセイ、英語の句読法

過去の経験を語るエッセイ

　このユニットでは皆さんの過去の経験を振り返るエッセイを書いてみましょう。そのために参考となるのが、例えば自伝や回想録に見られるスタイルです。自伝や回想録では著者のそれまでの人生全体、あるいは人生における特定のできごとについて、そこでの成功や失敗、さらにはその経験で得られた人生の教訓が語られます。いずれも１人称の主語による過去形の文章で語られます。過去の経験を語るエッセイでも、中心となるできごとや経験を説明した上で、それらが自分の人生にどのように重要だったかを述べます。

英語の句読法

　英語学習者が注意すべき点のひとつに、コロンやセミコロンといった英語特有の句読法があります。これらはエッセイ・ライティングでは大変便利なので、違いをしっかりと理解しておきましょう。

・コロン：直前の事柄の説明、具体的内容の列挙

　（例）There are three primary colours: red, blue, and yellow.

・セミコロン：意味的なつながりのある２文の接続

　（例）I'll make the decision tomorrow; things will be clearer then.

Summary in English on p. 87

About Japan: *Work with a partner and explain the picture.*
(Hint: What do you know about Soseki Natsume?)

10. Technology

In this unit, you are going to:
- write an email giving feedback about some technology
- study how to describe problems with computer technology

Warm-up

Picture Description

| 1. notes/front | 2. frustrated/computer |

Write one sentence describing each picture. Use the two words under each picture. You may change the forms.

1._____

2._____

Discussion

Discuss the following questions and write answers.

1. What do you use your smartphone for?

2. Which do you like better, texting messages or writing emails? Why?

3. What are the important things to consider when buying a smartphone?

4. What problems do people have with their smartphones?

5. How would your life change if you didn't have a smartphone?

Language Focus

A. Choose the best answer. Each one should be used only once.

From: JBowie@kafuwamail.com
To: customer.service@zuyudagate.com
Subject: RE: Feedback on your purchase

Dear Customer Service,

Thank you for your feedback (1)_____. Overall, I am satisfied with my new ZuyudaGate Elite laptop computer. I bought the computer because my old one was (2)_____. The new computer is much faster, and I am able to (3)_____ to the Internet much more quickly. However, I am not (4)_____ with the battery. It only seems to last eighty minutes, and the (5)_____ that the battery is low is usually too late. I bought the computer partly because I do a lot of (6)_____, and work during the time I am traveling. I would (7)_____ it if you could let me know whether such a short battery life is normal for this model.

Sincerely,

Jim Bowie

(a) commuting   (b) out-of-date   (c) satisfied   (d) appreciate
(e) connect   (f) request   (g) warning

B. Choose the best answer. Each one should be used only once.

1. The battery_____ very quickly when it's not plugged in.

2. The screen _____ when I'm watching a video.

3. New applications won't _____, so I can't use them.

4. The computer suddenly _____ when I'm working on something important.

5. Windows is slow to _____, so I have to wait for a long time.

(a) shuts down   (b) runs out   (c) boot   (d) keeps freezing   (e) install

Writing Example

Read and listen to the email message. Make notes in the table.

From: KeithWatts77@kafuwamail.com
To: SP Microphone Customer Service
Subject: RE: We welcome your review!

Dear Customer Service,

I bought the SP99 microphone to use it for my podcast recordings. I have been using a built-in mic on my laptop which ended up with poor sound quality. When I was looking for a new microphone, I found that the SP99 would best fit my purpose – I have seen a lot of positive comments and suggestions from my fellow amateur podcasters.

Overall, I am satisfied with my new mic – it is plug-and-play, with no special software installation on my laptop. The sound quality is far better than the built-in mic, producing almost no hissing noise. The only problem is that it picks up very small sounds, so I have to be careful not to make unnecessary noises while recording, which is a bit annoying. Could you let me know if there is a way for me to reduce the sensitivity?

Sincerely,

Keith Watts

Item	
Purchase reason	
Good point(s)	
Bad point(s)	
Request	

Preparing to Write

You are going to respond to the following email from your smartphone company. In your email, write ONE point that you are NOT satisfied with, and ONE request for the company.

From: Simon Bezos
To: studentXXX1533@kafuwamail.com
Subject: Thank you for choosing us!
Dear Customer,
Thank you for your recent purchase of a smartphone! We hope that you are satisfied with our product. As customer satisfaction is always our top priority, we would like to hear from you regarding how you rate the item you purchased. Thank you for your cooperation!
Best regards,
Simon Bezos (X Corporation, CEO)

Work in a pair. Ask and answer the questions about your own smartphone. (Think about cost, battery, size, speed, touch, display, apps, Wi-Fi).

1. What model do you own?
2. Why did you choose the model that you own?
3. What are some good points of your smartphone?
4. What are some bad points of your smartphone?
5. What request do you want to make?
6. How will you start your email?
7. How will you close your email?

Make notes in the table.

Item	
Purchase reason	
Good point(s)	
Bad point(s)	
Request	

Write your email on the next page.

60

Writing Practice

From: Simon Bezos

To: studentXXX1533@kafuwamail.com

Subject: RE: Thank you for choosing us!

_____

_____

_____

_____

_____

_____

_____

_____

_____

_____

_____

_____

_____

_____

Work in a pair. Pass your email messages to each other. Write a comment (e.g. "I have the same problem with my smartphone …").

_____

_____

_____

Resource Page

メールで意見や苦情を書く

　このユニットでは、商品やサービスに対する**意見**（feedback）や**苦情・クレーム**（complaints）のメールを書いてみましょう。この手のメールはフォーマルな文体で書かれることが多いので、書き出しは"Dear〜"、結びは"Sincerely"や"Yours truly"などの語が用いられます。

(1) 意見を書く

　最初にその商品やサービスについての良い点を記し、次に問題点を記します。以下、意見を書くのに役立つ表現をまとめます。

良い点	I think the … is very good. / I really like the …. / The … is excellent. / The … is very impressive.
問題点	以下のような表現を用いて、話の流れを切り替えます。 However, …. / The only problem is….

(2) 苦情を書く

・良い点は省き、本題である問題点から入ります。
　（例）I recently bought your product because it has been well reviewed. Unfortunately, there seems to be a problem with….
・感情を抑え、事実に基づき、丁寧かつ簡潔で的を射た説明を行います。
・相手への要望を必ず添えます。批判や非難が目的ではなく、商品やサービスの向上に寄与するような文面を心がけましょう。
　（例）Could you let me know if…? / Would it be possible to…?

Summary in English on p. 87

About Japan: *Work with a partner and explain the picture.*
(Hint: What do you know about Akihabara?)

11. Work

In this unit, you are going to:
- write an opinion essay
- study useful expressions for writing a structured opinion essay

Warm-up
Picture Description

1. young/windshield   2. serve/café

Write one sentence describing each picture. Use the two words under each picture. You may change the forms.

1._____

2._____

Discussion

Discuss the following questions and write answers.

1. What do you think makes a job enjoyable?

2. If you could work abroad for six months, where would you go, and why?

3. Which part-time jobs would you like to do, and why?

4. Describe the job you would like to do after graduation.

5. Which is more interesting, working for a small business or a big organization, and why?

Language Focus

A. Choose the best answer. Each one should be used only once.

> ### Is high pay more important than job satisfaction?
>
> I do not think that high pay is more important than job satisfaction, and I have two (1)_____ for supporting this position: morale and health. The (2)_____ point is that if you have an unsatisfying highly paid job, it is difficult to do it well because you will be unhappy. This will affect your morale when you are working. In contrast, (3)_____ you are interested in your work, (4)_____ you will be naturally motivated and try to do your best. The (5)_____ point is that doing a highly paid job without satisfaction can be bad for your health. Highly paid jobs are often stressful. While some level of stress is beneficial, if you are under a lot of pressure and unsatisfied, this can lead to problems (6)_____ high blood pressure and heart disease. Sometimes workers may turn to alcohol to relieve stress, which may damage areas of the body such as the liver. In (7)_____, I think that job satisfaction is more important than high pay. Although having a lot of money has some benefits, leading a fulfilled working life is far more important.

(a) such as	(b) then	(c) first	(d) second	(e) reasons
(f) conclusion	(g) if			

B. Choose the best answer. Each one should be used only once.

1. We were very _____ when we lost the contract to another firm.

2. The president's speech was designed to be _____.

3. The training day was very _____, so I slept deeply that night.

4. The employees were so _____ that they worked very well.

5. The financial results were very _____, so we were worried.

6. The employees were _____ because they had worked all night.

(a) tired	(b) tiring	(c) disappointed	(d) disappointing
(e) motivated	(f) motivating		

Writing Example

Read and listen to the essay. Make notes in the table.

> ### Should managements allow their employees to use company equipment for their private needs?
>
> I think managements should allow employees to use company equipment for their private needs based on two key reasons: It is almost impossible to stop employees from doing this; it may improve company morale and lead to greater productivity. While there are some risks associated with such a policy, I believe that they are outweighed by the practical realities and the benefits. Also, companies can take measures to reduce such risks.
>
> First, in terms of practical realities, it is almost impossible to stop employees using some company equipment for private needs; they have access to such a wide range of equipment including phones, computers, and photocopiers. With some of these, it may be difficult to separate work from private use. For example, employees may receive personal phone calls from family or friends, and they may sometimes need to make personal phone calls; an employee may have a sick daughter in bed at home and may wish to check on her.
>
> Second, allowing personal use of company equipment may help to boost morale. Working life can be stressful, and there are times when employees need to take breaks. During these times, they may wish to make phone calls, communicate with friends by email, or relax by surfing the Internet. In all these cases, employees are likely to be using company equipment. If they can use such company equipment, they are likely to have a more positive attitude, and so be more productive.
>
> In conclusion, I think that employees should be allowed to use company equipment for their private needs. I realize that there are some risks. For example, employees might waste too much time on computer games. However, a company management can issue practical guidelines, so that both the company and employees will benefit from the policy.

Writer's position	Agree / Disagree (Please circle)
Reason 1	Explanation/Example
Reason 2	Explanation/Example

Underline the thesis statement in the essay.

Preparing to Write

You are going to write an opinion essay on the following question:

In the past, some universities did not allow students to do part-time jobs during the terms or semesters. <u>Should students be allowed to do part-time jobs during university terms or semesters</u>? Why or why not? Give reasons or examples to support your answer.

Work in a pair. Discuss the following questions.

1. What kinds of part-time jobs do students do?

2. What do students learn from part-time jobs?

3. What are the problems of doing a part-time job during semesters?

4. Do you agree or disagree with the underlined question above?

5. Think of as many reasons to support your opinion as possible.

6. Look at the essay on p.65. Underline useful phrases that you can use in your essay.

7. Do you have any personal experiences of part-time work that you can write about?

Choose two reasons to support your position.

Your position	Agree / Disagree (Please circle)
Reason 1	Explanation/Example
Reason 2	Explanation/Example

Write a thesis statement for your essay.

_____

_____

Write your opinion essay on the next page.

Writing Practice

Should students be allowed to do part-time jobs during university terms or semesters?

_____

_____

_____

_____

_____

_____

_____

_____

_____

_____

_____

_____

_____

_____

_____

_____

_____

_____

_____

_____

_____

_____

_____

_____

_____

_____

_____

_____

_____

_____

Resource Page

Summary in English on p. 88

About Japan: *Work with a partner and explain the picture.*
(Hint: What do you know about Japanese business greetings?)

12. Famous Figures

In this unit, you are going to:
- write a short biography of a famous figure
- study useful words and phrases relating to people's life stories

Warm-up

Picture Description

1. wave/flag

2. woman/hand

Write one sentence describing each picture. Use the two words under each picture. You may change the forms.

1._____

2._____

Discussion

Discuss the following questions and write answers.

1. Which three Japanese historical figures do you admire, and why?

2. Which three international figures from abroad do you admire, and why?

3. What are some of the global issues we face today?

4. Name one famous person you studied that helped to reduce suffering in the world. Describe what she/he did.

5. How would you like to make a contribution to tackle global issues?

Language Focus

A. Choose the best answer. Each one should be used only once.

Sadako Ogata

Sadako Ogata was a diplomat, academic, and author; she was the first woman to become United Nations High Commissioner for Refugees (UNHCR). During her lifetime, she made a major contribution to improving the lives of countless refugees.

Ogata was born (1)_____ 16 September 1927. (2)_____ a young woman, she graduated with a degree in English literature from the University of the Sacred Heart, Tokyo. (3)_____, she studied at Georgetown University and received a master's degree in international relations. (4)_____, it was unusual for a Japanese woman to study abroad.

During the 1980s, Ogata taught international politics at Sophia University. Then, (5)_____ 1990, Ogata was appointed United Nations High Commissioner for Refugees. (6)_____ her time as High Commissioner she implemented effective strategies for helping refugees caused by the Gulf War, Yugoslav wars, and the Rwandan genocide. She was the High Commissioner (7)_____ 2001.

In October 2003, Ogata was appointed Head of the Japan International Cooperation Agency (JICA). (8)_____ she was head of JICA, the organization was involved in peace-building projects in Afghanistan and Mindanao. She retired from the organization in 2012, but continued to engage with humanitarian issues until her death in October 2019.

(a) until	(b) while	(c) after that	(d) as	(e) at that time	(f) on
(g) in	(h) during				

B. Choose the best answer. Each one should be used only once.

1. Florence Nightingale was _____ on 12 May 1820.

2. Hideyo Noguchi _____ of yellow fever in 1928.

3. After _____ the army, Chiune Sugihara became a diplomat.

4. On graduating from university, Shinobu Ishihara _____ the Japanese army.

5. In 2018, Tasuku Honjo was _____ a Nobel Prize for his work on cancer.

(a) awarded	(b) born	(c) leaving	(d) joined	(e) died

Writing Example

Read and listen to the biography. Make notes in the table.

Fridtjof Nansen

Fridtjof Nansen was an explorer, scientist, and diplomat; famous for his polar exploration as a young man, in later life he worked on behalf of refugees and displaced people, winning the Nobel Peace Prize in 1922. Born in 1861, Nansen lived during a time of polar exploration, as well as an age of great change that included the First World War and its aftermath.

In his early life, Nansen achieved fame as an explorer and scientist. As a boy, he was a very good skier and ice skater. As an adult, he became famous after spending three years trying to reach the North Pole from 1893 to 1896. In addition to being an explorer, he was also a scientist; he studied zoology for his first degree and received a doctorate for his work on the central nervous system of small sea animals.

In his later years, Nansen became a diplomat who worked on humanitarian issues. In 1920, he worked at the League of Nations, and was involved in the repatriation of 450,000 prisoners of war. In 1921, Nansen became the first High Commissioner for Refugees at the League of Nations. One of the main problems for refugees was that they often did not have internationally recognized identity papers; Nansen introduced the 'Nansen passport' which helped to protect refugees. In 1922, the Red Cross asked him to organize a relief programme for the starving people in the Russian famine of that period.

For his humanitarian work, Nansen received the Nobel Peace Prize in 1922. The prize money was used for humanitarian assistance in the Ukraine. Nansen continued to work for humanitarian causes until his death in 1930.

Name	
Year of birth	
Achievement/award	
Early years/life	
Later years/life	
Year of death	

Underline the thesis statement.

Preparing to Write

You are going to write a short biography of a historical figure who made a contribution to improving people's lives. Think about humanitarian issues, education, science, medicine, etc.

Write the names of some famous people who have changed the world for the better in the box.

| |
| |

Choose one of them, and discuss her/his life with another student using the questions below.

1. What is the person's name?

2. Why is she/he famous?

3. When was she/he born?

4. Where was she/he born?

5. What did she/he do in her/his early life?

6. What did she/he do in later life?

7. Did she/he receive any awards?

Name	
Year of birth	
Achievement/award	
Early years/life	
Later years/life	
Year of death	

Write a thesis statement for your essay.

_____

_____

Write your biographical essay on the next page.

Writing Practice

The Life of _____

_____

_____

_____

_____

_____

_____

_____

_____

_____

_____

_____

_____

_____

_____

_____

_____

_____

_____

_____

_____

_____

_____

_____

_____

_____

_____

Resource Page

Summary in English on p. 88

About Japan: *Work with a partner and explain the picture.*
(Hint: What you know about Chiune Sugihara?)

Review (2)

Look at the following writing tasks. Choose one email message and one essay. Circle the numbers that you choose and write about the topics. Refer back to the previous units for useful information.

Email Options

1. Write an email inviting some foreign students called Maria, Li Wei, and Amita to a concert at your university.
2. Write an email giving feedback on your university's online learning system (e.g. Moodle, Blackboard).

Essay Options

3. Write a descriptive essay about a foreign country or city that you would like to visit.
4. Write a reflective essay about some important events that you have experienced at university and what you learned from them.
5. Write an opinion essay about the following question: *Should high school students have to wear a uniform?*
6. Write a biographical essay about a famous painter, musician, or actor.

| From: |
| To: |
| Subject: |
| |

Essay: _____

_____

_____

_____

_____

_____

_____

_____

_____

_____

_____

_____

_____

_____

_____

_____

_____

_____

_____

_____

_____

_____

Notes

Please use these pages for completing your essays and making notes.

本書の英文を作成する際のメモ用に利用してください。

_____

_____

_____

_____

_____

_____

_____

_____

_____

_____

_____

_____

_____

_____

_____

_____

_____

_____

_____

_____

_____

_____

_____

Resource Pages (English)

Unit 1: Formal and Informal Email

In university, social, and working life, email is an important way of contacting others, and it is important to decide whether to use a formal or informal style. Informal styles can vary greatly, and include contractions (I've/We're), colloquialisms, and short phrases such as "Lunch 12:00 usual place?" Formal emails have a much more structured look and feel, usually with full sentences such as "Would you like to meet for lunch at 12:00 in the cafeteria?"

The openings and closings of an email can be used to identify whether an email is formal or informal. An informal email will use greetings such as "Hello" or "Hi" and first names. A more formal email will use "Dear" and family names (Mr. Smith).

Formal closings vary slightly from country to country. In the USA "Yours truly" and "Sincerely yours" are used in business emails. In the UK "Yours sincerely" is used to close an email where a family name is used in the opening. In a very formal email in which the opening is "Dear Sir/Madam" the email is closed with "Yours faithfully".

Some closings can be used in both formal and informal situations. Two commonly used closings are "Kind regards" and "Best wishes".

Unit 2: Structure for a single paragraph

Single paragraphs have a structure that can be used to perform many different functions. For example, a writer may want to argue a case, describe an event or landscape, consider a problem and its solution, define a concept, or explain a process. In the first half of this book, we focus on single paragraph writing (units 2,3,5 and 6).

For single-paragraph writing, the paragraph can be broken down into three main component parts: a topic sentence, a body of supporting sentences, and a concluding sentence. These constitute a beginning, a middle and an end to the paragraph.

In this unit, we focus on writing a descriptive paragraph. Here, the topic sentence is used to introduce what is to be described. An example of a topic sentence is "My favorite place in Kyoto is the Ryoanji rock garden". Then, the supporting sentences provide examples and details relating to the main topic. In this case, they provide the location and description of the site. Examples of supporting sentences are 'It is located in northwest Kyoto...' and 'The garden itself consists of fifteen different stones surrounded by gravel'. Finally, the concluding sentence finishes the paragraph. An example might be "In our modern world, a visit to the garden creates a feeling of serenity in our busy high-technology lives".

Note: In a paragraph, sentences should be next to each other. When using a keyboard, you should not hit return/enter after each sentence. Also, when using a keyboard, remember to indent your paragraph. Commonly used fonts are Times New Roman, Century, and Calibri. Font sizes are usually 12-point, and lines are usually either single-spaced or double-spaced.

Unit 3: Movie Reviews

Movie reviews can be found in most newspapers and magazines. They usually include the reviewer's opinion of the movie, supported by reasons. In this unit, you will write about your favorite movie, focusing on genre, theme, plot/story, and your reasons why you like the movie. In this kind of review, the present tense is usually used to describe the movie.

Most movies can be analysed using ideas of genre, theme, story, and plot. There are many types of genre. Some of the most popular are action movies, comedies (including romantic comedies, or romcoms), crime/gangster movies, horror movies, musicals, science fiction, and fantasy movies. The theme of the movie is its central unifying concept, such as love, death, power, survival, prejudice. The story describes the events in the movie in chronological order. However, the plot describes the events in the order they are seen. For example, many movies involve flashbacks to key past events.

Unit 4: Requests

Requests are often used in everyday life. For example, in class you might ask another student if you could borrow a pencil or eraser, and you might ask a teacher about changing the temperature of a room. There are many ways of phrasing requests, and it is important to choose the appropriate level of politeness.

When deciding on the politeness of the request statement, you need to consider two things: the difference in status between you and the receiver of the request, and the size of a request. For example, if you ask your teacher to open a window this is an easy request to someone in authority. If you ask your teacher to check a five-page application for a summer course, this is much more time-consuming for the teacher and a politer form of request is required.

There are many different request forms. Sometimes requests are phrased as statements, such as "I would be grateful if you could send me the meeting agenda". However, most requests are made using questions. The reason for this is that a request can be accepted or rejected. If the request is in the form of a question, if gives the receiver the clear option of politely accepting or rejecting it. Also, it clearly signals that the sender expects a reply.

Requests usually involve modal verbs (can, may, will), often in their past forms (could, would, might). A past form is politer, so that "Could I borrow a pen?" is slightly politer than "Can I borrow a pen?" To make a request even politer, extra phrases can be added. For example, "Would it be possible for you to...?", Would you be able to...?", "Do you think you would be able to...?". An example of a polite request statement is "I am wondering if you could...".

Unit 5: Problem-solution

Problem-solution paragraphs are practical pieces of writing in which a problem is described and a solution to it is proposed. The problem itself is usually introduced in a topic sentence, and further explained through supporting sentences. The solution is then proposed, and explained, with the paragraph being finished by a closing sentence.

Within the paragraph, the transition to a solution needs to be clearly made, and a variety of phrases can be used such as "To solve this problem, ...", "One way to solve this problem is..." or "A way of dealing with this problem is...". Modal verbs can also be used to soften proposed solutions such as "One way to solve the problem would be to..." or "One way to solve the problem might be to...".

Note: In explaining the problem through the supporting sentences, a variety of phrases may be used to indicate the consequences of a problem situation. Terms such as "Because of...", "As a result of..." or "Due to..." may be used.

Unit 6: Advice

The focus of this unit is on giving advice. Short articles giving advice can be seen in many magazines and newspapers. In the article, the author tries to give some useful tips on doing something. Many of these articles are in the form of lists.

As these kinds of articles are giving advice, they tend to use the pronoun "you", and contain modal verbs such as "should", "can" and "could". Phrases using modals such as "may/might want to" are often seen. Imperatives are also common. For example, "Choose healthy snacks such as nuts or dried fruits", or "Don't skip your breakfast" might be seen in tips for healthy eating. For advice, "had better" is not usually used because it can be a warning.

Article titles giving advice often include terms such as "ways" or "tips". With the term "tips", gerunds such as "working" or "staying" are also common. Examples of titles are "10 tips for relieving stress" or "5 tips to relieve stress". With "ways", the infinitive can be used ("10 ways to relieve stress") or the gerund ("10 ways of relieving stress"). Other titles could be "Relieving stress" or "How to relieve stress". Note that "ways" collocates with "of" but not "for", "tips" collocates with "for" but not "of".

Unit 7: Making Invitations by Email and Responding to Them

When making an invitation by email, it is important to state the event and to make the invitation in the appropriate register. If the event is soon, the present continuous is often used (e.g. "I'm holding a birthday party on the last Saturday of this month). Invitations are often in the form of questions (e.g. "Would you like to come?") but can also be in the form of statements (e.g. I am writing on behalf of _____ to invite you to speak at our annual symposium). "Do you want to _____?" is less formal than "Would you like to _____?". With close friends, email communication may be very short, an example being "Mario's tonight, 6:00?"

When accepting an invitation, the responder usually expresses thanks ("Thank you for the invitation") and clearly states her/his acceptance: "I would love to come to the party" or more informally, "That sounds great"). When declining an invitation, the responder usually expresses thanks ("Thank you for the invitation"), declines with a reason: ("Unfortunately, I have previous commitment on that day" or more informally, "I'm sorry, I can't make it"), and expresses good wishes: "Have a great party".

Unit 8: Structuring an Essay

Make sure your essay has a title that makes it clear to the reader what the essay is about. Capitalize all nouns, pronouns, adjectives, verbs and adverbs. Do not capitalize conjunctions and small words (e.g. and, or, to), except for the first word. (e.g. "The Diverse Population of Montreal")

The introduction is the first paragraph. It includes the thesis statement, which expresses the main ideas of the essay.

The body of the essay consists of two or three paragraphs and provides the details supporting the main theme of the essay. Each paragraph should be about a topic related to the main theme.

The conclusion is the last paragraph, which summarizes the essay. It restates the main idea, comments on, and finishes the essay.

Unit 9: Reflective Writing

In this unit, you are going to write about personal experience. This kind of writing can be seen in autobiographies and memoirs. In an autobiography, an author tries to describe important elements of his/her life, sharing in his successes and failures and lessons learned from them. A memoir is more focused on particular events in an author's life rather than his/her whole life. Some fictional stories are very autobiographical. Memoirs and autobiographies are nearly always written in the past tense and in the first person.

Think carefully about punctuation, especially colons and semicolons. A colon (:) usually introduces an item or list. For example, "There are three primary colours: red, blue, and yellow." A semicolon (;) can replace a period if two sentences are closely linked. For example, "I'll make the decision tomorrow; things will be clearer then."

Unit 10: Feedback Emails and Complaint Emails

When giving feedback it is customary to give the good points first, and then describe the negative points. When stating positive points, there are a variety of phrases that can be used. Examples of these are: "I think the … is very good", "I really like the …", "The … is excellent", "The … is very impressive". When giving negative feedback, it is usually necessary to signal the change from positive points to negative points through a linking phrase such as "However, …" or "The only problem is…".

Complaint emails are similar to feedback emails, but are not usually in reply to a request email. They come to the negative point much more quickly, and there is no need to state the positive points. For example: "I recently bought your product because it has been well reviewed. Unfortunately, there seems to be a problem with…". It is important to write a polite, concise and to-the-point message, based on the problem you are experiencing. Also, always add what you would like the company to do. Among some useful phrases for making a request are "Could you let me know if…?" and "Would it be possible to…? Remember that you are not writing to criticize or blame them, but to remedy a problem or help them make better products/services.

Both feedback and complaint emails tend to be formal in nature, starting with "Dear…" and closing with "Sincerely", "Yours truly", etc.

Unit 11: Opinion Essays

The benefits of writing opinion essays are that they help you to clarify and order ideas. Although an opinion essay tends to be seen in academic life, other forms of writing often require the production of arguments. In non-academic life, we have to decide courses of action to take, so that arguing a case is an important life skill.

With an opinion essay there are always ways of arguing for and against the opinion that you hold. The introduction should contain a thesis statement in which you clearly state your opinion and introduce your reasons for holding this position. An example of a thesis statement is "I think that high school students should wear a school uniform for the following reasons: It creates a sense of belonging; it creates equality among students." The body of the essay is then used to develop the reasons written in the thesis statement.

When you are writing an opinion essay, you are basically stating that your arguments for your position outweigh the arguments against it. You may wish to address such arguments as part of your conclusion.

Unit 12: Biographical Essay

A biography is an account of someone's life. Its length can vary from a short summary to several books. In this unit, we focus on writing a short summary of a famous person, similar to biographies that can be seen in encyclopedias. Short biographies in the form of obituaries can also be seen in newspapers and magazines when famous people die.

Usually the introductory paragraph of a biography will contain a thesis statement that outlines the life and achievements of the person. This is followed by the paragraphs of the body, which break down the person's life into key periods. Finally, the concluding paragraph is used to highlight key points and finish the essay.

Biographies usually include various time phrases, such as 'after', 'before', 'during' and 'until', which are the language focus of this unit. Because they are about the past, biographies are nearly always written in the past tense.

Photographs

Shutterstock

p1. 415325905
p1. 1077839543
p6. 517861963
p7. 1317925727
p7. 1370889146
p8. 1139557301
p9. 506751340
p12. 1274739874
p13. 535946224
p13. 216781504
p15. 786563389
p18. 1241522563
p19. 1629602980
p19. 407807179
p22. 625928870
p24. 1464710273
p25. 341987081
p25. 1361622428
p27. 1019630131
p27. 238519603
p30. 1526458241
p31. 404379568
p31. 676559059
p36. 1311176495
p39. 764943697
p39. 658918132
p44. 31120027
p45. 792301468
p45. 1023588598
p50. 181358573
p51. 1302192277
p51. 174906893
p57. 1079701088
p57. 1017688288
p62. 1188863533
p63. 1564350646
p63. 1061566172
p68. 1061269235

p71. 517563670
p71. 351822401
p74. 332234906

Public Domain

P56. Soseki Natsume
P71. Fridtjof Nansen

テキストの音声は、弊社 HP　https://www.eihosha.co.jp/
の「テキスト音声ダウンロード」のバナーからダウンロードできます。
また、下記 QR コードを読み込み、音声ファイルをダウンロードするか、
ストリーミングページにジャンプして音声を聴くことができます。

Effective Writing for Global Communication
—Email, Paragraph, and Essay
グローバル・コミュニケーションのためのライティング
—E メール・パラグラフ・エッセイ

2020 年 10 月 1 日　初　版　　　　　　2023 年 10 月 20 日　第 3 刷

　　　　　　　　　　榎　田　一　路
　　　著　　者 ©Ｗａｌｔｅｒ　Ｄａｖｉｅｓ
　　　　　　　　　　田　北　冬　子

　　発 行 者　佐　々　木　　　元

発 行 所　株式
　　　　　会社　英　　宝　　社

〒 101-0032 東京都千代田区岩本町 2-7-7
電話 03-5833-5870　FAX03-5833-5872
https://www.eihosha.co.jp/

ISBN 978-4-269-32012-3 C1082
組版・印刷・製本／日本ハイコム株式会社